ROWLEY REVISITED

ANTHONY H. PAGE

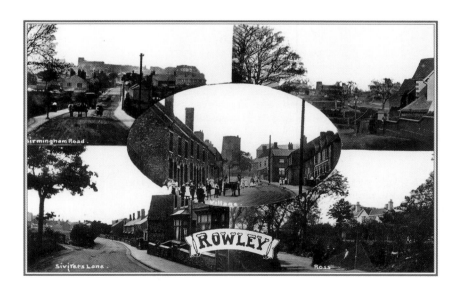

SUTTON PUBLISHING

Sutton Publishing Limited
Phoenix Mill · Thrupp · Stroud
Gloucestershire · GL5 2BU

First published 2005

Copyright © Anthony H. Page, 2005

Title page: A multi-view postcard of Rowley.
(Angela Ruckwood)

British Library Cataloguing in Publication Data
A catalogue record for this book is available from the
British Library.

ISBN 0-7509-3090-X

Typeset in 10.5/13.5 Photina.
Typesetting and origination by
Sutton Publishing Limited.
Printed and bound in England by
J.H. Haynes & Co. Ltd, Sparkford.

THE BLACK COUNTRY SOCIETY

The Black Country Society is proud to be associated with **Sutton Publishing** of Stroud. In 1994 the society was invited by Sutton Publishing to collaborate in what has proved to be a highly successful publishing partnership, namely the extension of the *Britain in Old Photographs* series into the Black Country. In this joint venture the Black Country Society has played an important role in establishing and developing a major contribution to the region's photographic archives by encouraging society members to compile books of photographs of the area or town in which they live.

The first book in the Black Country series was *Wednesbury in Old Photographs* by Ian Bott, launched by Lord Archer of Sandwell in November 1994. Since then nearly seventy Black Country titles have been published. The total number of photographs contained in these books is in excess of 13,000, suggesting that the whole collection is probably the largest regional photographic survey of its type in any part of the country to date.

This voluntary society was founded in 1967 as a reaction to the trends of the late 1950s and early '60s. This was a time when the reorganisation of local government was seen as a threat to the identity of individual communities and when, in the name of progress and modernisation, the industrial heritage of the Black Country was in danger of being swept away.

The general aims of the society are to stimulate interest in the past, present and future of the Black Country, and to secure at regional and national levels an accurate understanding and portrayal of what constitutes the Black Country and, wherever possible, to encourage and facilitate the preservation of the Black Country's heritage.

The society, which now has over 2,500 members worldwide, organises a yearly programme of activities. There are five venues in the Black Country where evening meetings are held on a monthly basis from September to April. In the summer months, there are fortnightly guided evening walks in the Black Country and its green borderland, and there is also a full programme of excursions further afield by car. Details of all these activities are to be found on the society's website, **www.blackcountrysociety.co.uk**, and in *The Blackcountryman*, the quarterly magazine that is distributed to all members.

PO Box 71 · Kingswinford · West Midlands DY6 9YN

CONTENTS

INTRODUCTION

Why is Rowley called Regis?

by

David Hickman, vice-chairman of
Rowley and Blackheath Local Interest Group

Why were the village and then the surrounding area given the name Rowley Regis? This is one of the first questions that people who are interested in the history of this area often ask. Answers that always seem readily available include 'it once belonged to the king', or 'there was a hunting lodge there belonging to the king'. If these answers are correct, then which king was he, when and where did he live, and how and why was the town named?

Unfortunately these questions are not so easy to answer. The early history and any records that are available are not that easy to find, translate or understand. In some cases Rowley history can only be at the best comparison and speculation. In order to begin this quest, the geography of the area needs to be examined, as in many ways this defines the history.

Many thousands of years ago a large ridge was formed by volcanic activity, stretching from Sedgley to Northfield, with its highest point at Turner's Hill, approximately 876ft above sea level. This ridge developed fertile valleys that are fed by the watershed from the slopes, large forests, plateau lands and heath lands where the soil was poor, and the area around the summits which was usually rocky.

However, this area cannot be said to have been the best place for a settlement. According to the Domesday survey of Staffordshire of 1086 the substantial covering of forests appeared more welcoming to deer, boar and wolves than to its population. But people still travelled through the forests, across and around the ridge, stopping at the springs and streams for water, and if they wanted a secure place to spend the night, the summits of the ridges were the best available places to camp. Ancient Britons and Celts must have passed through and lived in this area. If Rowley is compared with Clent, one of its neighbouring villages, there is a general similarity in the geography.

The history books say that the Romans did not venture this far into the south Staffordshire area 2,000 years ago, as it had large forested valleys, and warlike Celts on every hill. But local historians believe the opposite is true, with possible

Roman camps and battles all over the Rowley area, as several Roman finds have been unearthed over the years. The Romans were probably attracted by the hard rock of the Rowley hills, as the legacy of quarrying can be seen in the landscape.

When the Roman central administration left the country, it was policed by a mercenary force employed by the Romans. Celts and other indigenous peoples took the opportunity to return to their pre-Roman tribes and leaders. The Rowley area was probably part of the Welsh kingdom of Powys; when the Roman rulers withdrew, the borderlands, or March area, was given to the sons of King Mawn or Lago ap Brochfael. This area was divided into three small sub-kingdoms, but all under the name of Pengwern.

After many turbulent years of upheaval, fighting and changes of ownership the three sub-kingdoms were defeated by Anglo-Saxon tribes in the sixth century. One of the tribes, the Iclingas, gradually extended its power, amalgamating the kingdoms in and around the Midlands. It eventually became known by the territory it conquered, and evolved into the kingdom of Mercia. Creoda became its first identifiable king, and claimed he was a descendant of Woden, the principal Anglo-Saxon god. The Britons and the Celts were now under the lordship of Anglo-Saxons, but did they believe in the same pagan gods? Many Britons and Celts would have been Christian converts. Did the features of the rock formation now known as The Hailstone become the first religious site in Rowley? It is said that these rock formations were the remains of battles between these pagan gods. Perhaps this is the main reason why early paths came across the Rowley hills and not around them.

The comparisons and links with Clent and later other villages are not accidental. When the Anglo-Saxons became the dominant power in the country, major changes took place. Stability in the villages would mean that agriculture could flourish with a new lord of the manor in charge. It has not been possible to track down any information about the early Saxon landowners in the Rowley area; only records of the kings and earls who ruled Mercia survive. However, during this era several new administrative changes took place. The large kingdoms were split into new smaller shires, with a shire-reeve (later known as a sheriff) in charge of collecting the taxes for the king. Rowley was now part of the Seisdon Hundred, in Staffordshire.

The villages of Swinford (Staffordshire) and Clent and Tardebigge (Worcestershire) formerly belonged to the monastery and church at Worcester. They were purchased by the Deacon Æthelsige, one of the king's councillors, from King Æthelred for £200 of silver, for the perpetual possession of the Worcester monastery. This is the first major clue to the royal ownership of these Mercian villages.

After the death of King Æthelred in 1016, his son Edmund Ironside claimed the throne. There then followed hard fighting between the English and the Danes under the command of Cnut in and around the Rowley area. Æuic, the then Sheriff of Staffordshire, seized the lands with all the rents and tax payable, even though some were in Worcestershire. It is thought that the villages in the Rowley area could have been owned by the Shrewsbury family of Godgyfu of Mercia who married the Earl Leofric of Mercia in 1030. She is much better known as Lady Godiva.

Many local villages and hamlets (including Rowley), rivers and streams were given new names during the early Anglo-Saxon era. The name Rowley derived from the Anglo-Saxon for rough woodland or clearing, Ruh leah. This is a clue to its place in the landscape. Perhaps there were people living and working in the clearing on top of this wooded hill or was it a place or landmark en route to somewhere? By the mid-eleventh century Rowley was surrounded by Danish lands, but did the locals resist these neighbours or were the boundaries observed by all parties?

Land changed hands regularly. Lords of the manors would have owned lands in several shires and hundreds. Taxes and rents proved difficult for the shire-reeves to collect and justify, and the constant fighting between kingdoms and nations was putting a drain on the resources of the county. Land ownership meant wealth and power. During these troubled times Clent and probably Rowley were given to the Monastery of Worcester, but how Clent managed to break away from Danish control, I have not yet discovered. However, the fighting between the families and followers of Edmund and Cnut would mean the lands at Rowley and Clent were not given to the monastery of Worcester straight away. Following the short and unpopular reign of King Cnut's sons, Harold (Harefoot) and Hardecanute, the lands were taken back into royal ownership by another son of the old Anglo-Saxon king, Æthelred, who returned from exile in Normandy to claim the throne of England, Edward the Confessor. This could be another clue to why the terms Kings and Regis were given to the villages of Kingswinford and Rowley Regis, but if this is true, why were Clent and Tardebigge not also part of these lands?

King Edward now held Kingswinford, Penkridge, the woods of Enville and Cippemore, Clent (which probably included Rowley) and Tardebigge. So most of the lands around Rowley were owned by very high-ranking members of the English gentry or the royal family. The Norman influence on the king, and in fact all of England, created a stable period, in reality paving the way for the Norman Conquest of 1066 led by William, Duke of Normandy. The Normans had a different way of life, language and loved to hunt. They acquired and set aside vast areas of heath and woodlands, known as royal forests, which were owned and managed by the crown for hunting purposes.

After the conquest William, now king, took possession of all the royal estates. However, the Anglo-Saxons did not give way easily, and rebellions were many and bloody. A battle was fought at the town of Stafford, where the rebels were defeated, but this was not enough to stamp out resistance in the area. So early in 1070 William returned to show the extent of his power, and took fearful revenge on the people of Yorkshire and then Staffordshire. Little is known of what happened on these two campaigns, but the destruction of Staffordshire was so great that, according to contemporary records, 'men young and old, women and children wandered as far as the Abbey of Evesham in the quest of a morsel of bread'.

More than fifteen years later at the time of the Domesday survey many local communities were no longer tilling the land, and were recorded as merely 'Wasta est' (it is wasted); in fact about one-fifth of Staffordshire was classed as wasted. The properties of the rebellious Earls Edwin and Morcar in Yorkshire and Staffordshire were either given to the king's most trusted followers, or were added to the king's own lands and were known as Terra Regis (king's land). Could this be the first time that the designation Regis was used to denote royal lands and property; was Rowley about to be broken away from Clent?

What was left of south Staffordshire was now a wasteland. However, the woodlands were soon to become the saving grace for the area, as one of the king's passions was hunting, so he introduced new and vigorously enforced laws to expand and protect the royal forests and game, particularly boar and deer. Rowley must have still been part of Clent, because the Domesday survey did not list it separately. But the area around Rowley was either owned by the king or by William Fitz Ansc]]ulf. Dudley was emerging as a large town with a stone castle, a base for the Norman lord. The royal forests covered the majority of southern Staffordshire, so it is only right to say Rowley must have been part of the forest.

The royal forests were not necessarily covered with trees. It is estimated that only one-fifth of the forests were woodland. The rest was composed of a variety of landscapes, including heath and wasteland. The forest was a tract of land which was subject to the Forest Laws. The king and the royal household alone had the right to hunt in these areas, and special officials were appointed to look after them and bring the poachers to justice. Many a poacher sat in the dungeons of the manorial castles awaiting punishment for as little as snaring a rabbit to feed his family. The new laws stipulated that a poacher could have a hand chopped off, be blinded or have his testicles severed. In reality poachers were usually fined, imprisoned, outlawed or pardoned. The Pipe Rolls show that by 1150 the main effect of the Forest Laws was to provide revenue for the king.

The Norman lords were keen to introduce another custom very similar to the Forest Laws imposed by the king – the right to warrene. This meant that an area of land could be fenced off so that the nobility could hunt small game – foxes, hares, wild cats, badgers, squirrels, martens, otters, partridges, pheasants and rabbits – on their own lands. Rabbits originated in southern Europe and were introduced into England by the Normans in the twelfth century. At first they did not take well to the English climate, but their keepers, or warreners, pampered them, gave them specially made shelters, food and protection from predators. Eventually the rabbits acclimatised and colonised the larger warrens. These were zealously guarded by their keepers, who were employed by the lord of the manor to care for and protect them from gangs of armed poachers. Warreners lived in fortified lodges, usually built on high, dry-soiled areas such as heathlands within a warren, so that they could keep a look-out for poachers.

This could be another clue to the history of Rowley. Within the Rowley area are lands called Warrens Hall Park, and high up on the Rowley Hills is a farm called Warrens Hall Farm. Is this where the Norman lord of the manor exercised his right to warrene? Could the humble rabbit be a large part of our heritage? Was the hunting lodge mentioned earlier perhaps a warrener's?

Rowley was probably still included in the lands associated with Clent until the late twelfth century, because they were still taxed as one unit until 1170 when the village was named for the first time separately. The tax for Clent and Rowley together was 13s 4d. When Rowley paid its own tax, it was only 6s 2d. At less than half the original tax, it was recorded in the Sheriff's Rolls. Unfortunately the separation was short lived, as in 1195 Rowley was again joined to Clent to provide more money in taxation for the king.

Events at Dudley had moved on apace. William Fitz Ansculf had passed the ownership of the manor through his daughter to Fulk Paynel, who in turn passed it through his grand-daughter to the first John de Somery. In 1205 King John sold the manors of Clent, Kingswinford and Mere to Ralph, the son of John de Somery, who was by then the lord of the manor at Dudley Castle, in exchange for the manor of Wolverhampton and 100 marks, or £66 13s 4d and a yearly rent of £21 13s 4d. This rent was to be paid by the three manors. The same King John was known to have spent many days hunting in the royal forests around Kinver, as well as staying at the Hunting Lodge at Stourton Castle. The manors of Clent and Rowley were passed from generation to generation until they finally came to another John de Somery, who died without leaving an heir. The manors were then divided between his sisters Margaret (1290–1384), who married John de Sutton, who became the Lord of Dudley Castle, and Joan. One half was called Rowley Somery and the other Rowley Regis after the king.

So have we finally come to the reason why the village of Rowley was called Rowley Regis? If lands were left without an heir in medieval times they were transferred to the ownership of the king. So was there a conflict between these sisters? Did the king step in and sort out the dispute? Was this the only way to stop the power struggle? The answers to these questions are not known. The lands roughly adjacent to the church and glebe lands around Blackheath became Rowley Regis. Rowley Regis then stayed in the Manor of Dudley because Margaret de Somery married John de Sutton, ancestor of the Earls of Dudley, and continued living in Dudley Castle. For many years the whole area was in the hands of the Earls of Dudley, but gradually over time much of the glebe land was sold off.

In the mid-nineteenth century Lord Ward was lord of the manor of Rowley Regis and owned much of the village, and the Duke of Sutherland held the manor of Rowley Somery, where he had a large estate and mines.

1

Around & About

A young Tony Crump gazes out towards Portway Farm from its adjacent fields,
1963. It was still a fully working farm at the time, with pigs, cattle and horses, and
had occupied the site for centuries. A traditional haystack can be seen on the left.
(Derek Crump)

A view from Birmingham Road, looking towards Rowley Village with the third St Giles' Church on the horizon. The Sir Robert Peel public house can be seen in the middle distance, with the large house and grounds belonging to the Mackmillan family. The houses in Bell End can be seen on the right-hand side, which pre-dates the construction of the large council house estate. *(Author's Collection)*

Rowley Village, with the post office on the left-hand side, *c.* 1900. Fading into the distance is the housing that disappeared in the 1950s. *(Author's Collection)*

Rowley Village, at the junction with Bell End, looking towards Blackheath, *c.* 1920. The Britannia Inn is the large building on the right, standing next to the entrance to the park of the same name. *(Malcolm Whitehouse)*

Halesowen & Hasbury Co-operative Society, branch no. 15, in the early 1960s. Situated next to the Britannia Inn in Rowley Village, it later became a domestic appliance centre, before making way for the present convenience stores, including the post office, until the latter was closed in 2004. *(Ned Williams)*

Two views of Dudley Road, Springfield, looking towards Dudley. Bayley's post office, a well-known landmark, is visible on the left-hand side of each picture. *(Author's Collection) Above*: The old cottages still stand at the top of Springfield Lane, and Knowle Colliery is just visible on the right, *c.* 1920.
Below: The effects of modernisation are plain to see, 1986. The pit has been replaced by the Crendon Road housing estate, and access to Springfield Lane has been opened up. The Royal Oak public house is in the middle distance. *(CHAS)*

The junction where Uplands Avenue joins Mincing Lane seen from Oldbury Road, 1986. It is in a very pleasant and popular residential area. The corner shop ceased trading after many years early in the twenty-first century, and has been re-converted to a dwelling place. *(CHAS)*

With the explosion in demand for housing in the years after the Second World War, the waste ground known locally as the Quack was developed by the Local Authority and included these blocks of flats. Named after local landmarks, they were called St Giles' Court and Ridgeacre Court. Between the flats Uplands Avenue can be seen, and in the distance is Langley. *(CHAS)*

The rural setting above Ross, where it joins Siviter's Lane, *c.* 1900. *(Author's Collection)*

A view of Siviter's Lane from roughly outside the school, *c.* 1925. The housing on the left was occupied by the more affluent members of Rowley society such as doctors, lawyers and shopkeepers. *(Author's Collection)*

A view from the tower of St Giles' Church, overlooking Barnsley's garage, 1980s. In the foreground it is backed by (left to right) Rowley Labour Club, the Scout headquarters and the Parish Church Hall. The land falls off towards Old Hill and Brierley Hill, with the playing fields of Rowley Regis Grammar School in the middle distance. *(Christine Brettell)*

The view from Britannia Road towards Rowley Village, with Park Court flats in the centre and Bell End on the right, 1970s. The shops and houses are awaiting demolition, and in recent years have been replaced by Carillon Gardens. Built over the old mine workings, the houses had been subjected to years of subsidence, and many were held up by large iron tie-bars. *(Vera Guest)*

The corner shop standing at the junction of Club Buildings and Hawes Lane, with Hawes Lane Methodist Chapel just visible on the far left, 1986. Shortly after this photograph was taken these properties were demolished in order to make way for a road straightening and widening scheme, which, incidentally, has never taken place. *(CHAS)*

A rare photograph of the Bull's Head public house in Hawes Lane, late nineteenth century (see also page 25). It was here that T.W. Williams set up a small brewery, which sold beer in many other pubs in Rowley and the surrounding area. Business was so good that a larger brewery was built in nearby Tippity Green, where it continued until 1927. *(Author's Collection)*

Miss Mary Hall, who was born in 1906 and later became Mrs Raybould, outside her place of employment, the Rowley Gas Company, in Birmingham Road, *c.* 1925. The company had its Gas Works at the bottom of Powke Lane. *(Enid Bissell)*

The Old Pear Tree public house in Mincing Lane, which was extensively modernised until it was recently demolished to make way for new housing, *c.* 1936. Irene Brookes and Jean Yardley are the girls in this view. Local children used to play in the old cow shed, swinging from the beams. *(Bob Grosvenor)*

Dudley Road, Springfield, from outside Bayley's post office looking back towards Rowley, 1986. The original entrance to Springfield Working Men's Club can be seen on the left. The old housing stock seen here was demolished shortly after this picture was taken. *(CHAS)*

The Hailstone Inn, Springfield, at the top of Springfield Lane, opposite the post office, 1986. It was named after the legendary rocky outcrop that also gave its name to the quarry. *(CHAS)*

The summit of Turner's Hill where it joins with Oakham Road, with the Wheatsheaf public house on the right, in the 1970s. *(CHAS)*

The summit of Turner's Hill from the back garden of 36 Lye Cross Road, Tividale, May 1963. No. 36 was a brand new council house, that with others in the road was built on the site of a Second World War anti-aircraft gun emplacement. On Turner's Hill, which is approximately 876ft above sea level, is the old water tower and an early version of a radio/television/telephone mast, the twenty-first century version of which is now visible for miles. The large house and the smaller cottages on the skyline were still inhabited at this time. *(Derek Crump)*

The Yew Tree public house was a favourite drinking place of the employees of T.W. Lench, as it was situated just outside the factory premises in Carnegie Road. It is shown here in the latter stages of its demolition, in the 1980s. *(CHAS)*

Looking towards Dudley from Allsop's Quarry, mid-1980s. The corner shop and houses in Tippity Green are in the middle distance. *(David Westwood)*

The Royal Oak public house, Dudley Road, Springfield, at the extreme edge of Rowley Regis, on the boundary with Dudley, 1969. *(CHAS)*

A more recent picture of the Bull's Head public house, Hawes Lane, Rowley Regis, 1982 (see also page 20). In recent years it has changed its name to Chaplins. *(Terry Price)*

Above: Decimus Gaunt welcomes patrons to the Old Bush Revived public house, in Powke Lane, early twentieth century. Well known throughout town, he was the ancestor of Percival Gaunt who founded the well-respected family-run business of funeral directors. *(Betty Johnson)*
Below: The same establishment after some alterations, 1982. *(Terry Price)*

The top of Turner's Hill, when traffic was allowed to travel between the two deep quarries, near the junction with Oakham Road, 1970s. *(CHAS)*

Rowley Village, prior to the total redevelopment of the area near the parish church, with the post office on the left. The old cottages are clearly visible, as are the junction with Siviter's Lane and the shops on the corner, which included Goode's Stores and the coal merchant. *(Malcolm Whitehouse)*

The rural setting of Throne Farm, the largest in the area, with the herd of Friesians grazing peacefully. Situated off Throne Road, the farm comprised more than 100 acres. It was purchased in 1920 by the Skidmore family, who farmed both livestock and vegetables, although they never kept pigs. *(Graham Beasley)*

A view from the rough path which started from Brickhouse Farm/Moor Lane, winter 1955. It wandered up through the field and old quarry workings until it ended in Hawes Lane between the old Church School and Barnsley's Garage, opposite the Ward Arms public house. Just beyond the picture to the right was an old cottage that was in front of the Labour Club and the Scout room of the 1st Rowley Scouts. The bank on the left was swallowed by the grounds of Rowley Regis Grammar School, later Rowley College. *(Derek Crump)*

The original Portway Hall was built in the third quarter of the seventeenth century for the yeoman farmer Johnson family, and was originally constructed as a half-timbered building. Over the years it had sunk over 20ft from its original level, probably owing to mine workings. After two centuries it was extended and developed into this structure. Its grounds stretched for some 250 acres. This view was taken shortly before the building was demolished in 1979. *(CHAS)*

Oakham Road possessed many fine houses, this one being Oakham House. With fine views over Dudley Golf Course it commanded a prime position. However, the ravages of time and exposure took their toll, and the house was demolished in 1969. Here it is seen during the demolition period. *(CHAS)*

The exterior and interior of Hawthorns public house, on the corner of Ross and Shepherd's Fold, April 1928. *(CHAS)*

Club Buildings, off Hawes Lane, awaiting demolition, with the graveyard of St Giles' Church in the background, 1970s. *(Author's Collection)*

Hawes Lane, towards the parish church, with the Methodist Chapel on the left, late 1940s. The end of Club Buildings can be seen next to the parked van, with the old cottages still standing. *(Author's Collection)*

The Sir Robert Peel public house, situated at the very bottom of Rowley Village, almost at the junction with Mackmillan Road, *c. 1970*. The pub will long be remembered for the very lifelike three-dimensional painting of a man up a ladder seemingly pasting an advertisement for Ansells beer on the side of the pub, which was visible from a long distance when descending Rowley Hill. It is said that at one time the bar was in the room to the left, while the room to the right was used as a butcher's shop. *(Author's Collection)*

The shop and house at the corner of Rowley Village and Siviters Lane, prior to redevelopment. Note the precarious angle of the two adjacent properties, caused by subsidence from the many mine workings underneath the hill. *(Mary Cutler)*

The land which used to house the reservoir, off Bell End and Newhall Road, has been sold off for residential development. This is the entrance to the site before the large housing estate was built, November 1968. *(CHAS)*

The rear view of Rose Cottage, 15 Church Road, Rowley Regis, adjacent to the top of Park Avenue. Over the years it had been the home to a number of families, either as owners or tenants, and census records indicate that it had been a boarding school at one time. *(Graham Beasley)*

Rowley Regis Conservative and Unionist Club, in Hawes Lane, opposite the site of the Methodist Chapel, 1968. The driveway on the far left used to be the entrance to Rowley Regis Grammar School, later taken over as an outpost of Dudley Technical College, which is due to close in the summer of 2005. *(CHAS)*

The remaining houses in Springfield Lane, looking up towards the shops and the Hailstone Inn, 1967. *(CHAS)*

The junction of Powke Lane with Ross, with the premises of John Tooth next to the traffic lights, late 1980s. The entrance to the builder's yard can be seen at the rear of the premises. Shortly after this picture was taken the cottages were demolished to make better access. The Hawthorns public house is just visible on the left. *(John Tooth)*

Yew Tree Lane, looking towards Powke Lane, in 1968, built on land reclaimed from a mining area known as The Totnalls. The old cottage just visible through the trees is believed to be the original meeting house of a group who went on to form Birmingham Road Methodist Church. *(CHAS)*

A rare photograph, taken in 1921, of part of the exterior of Rowley Hall, demolished in the latter part of the twentieth century. Perhaps one of the most significant buildings in the area, it has a history going back to the Gunpowder Plot of 1605, and was the home of many of the more influential members of Rowley society, including mine owners. *(Tony Collins)*

The farmhouse and yard of Old Portway Farm, situated on Portway Hill, June 1969 (see also page 13). *(CHAS)*

A solitary man stands by the old lamp-post at the top of Rowley Village, where the road veers right into Church Road, on the morning following the fire at St Giles' Church on 18 June 1913. *(Malcolm Whitehouse)*

The paddling pool and boating lake in Britannia Park, with the houses of Bell End and Rowley Village and the rear of the Britannia Inn in the background, 1940s. *(Malcolm Whitehouse)*

The houses in Club Row have now been demolished, and although the area is overgrown with weeds, we can still catch a glimpse of the Ebenezer Chapel (Ruston's Chapel) off Hawes Lane, 1968. The corner shop, seen on page 20, is on the left. The cottages leading up to the Ward Arms were pulled down shortly after they were caught on film. *(CHAS)*

The old houses situated in the grounds of ARC quarries prior to their demolition, 22 January 1984. The area had been earmarked for the future siting of the massive radio/telephone transmission towers. *(Derek Crump)*

2

Schooldays

Miss Maud Westwood, the revered head teacher of Siviter's Lane School, is seen preparing a group of her charges for a holiday to Paris in 1953. (*Maud Shaw*)

David Field, Gareth Shaw, Edward Green, James Taylor and Raymond Dickens made up the Sandwell Jubilee Quiz Junior Champions in 1980. Representing Blackheath Junior School (Powke Lane) they beat Holly Hedge Junior School, West Bromwich, in the final held in West Bromwich Town Hall. *(Author's Collection)*

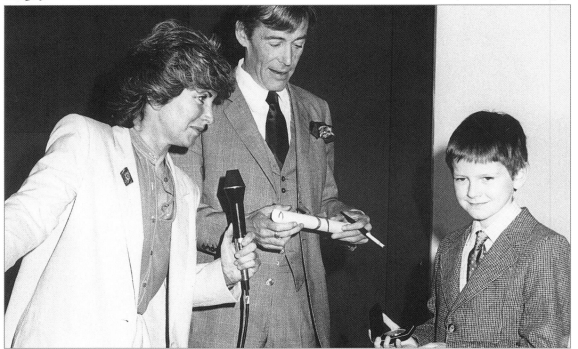

James Taylor again, this time in April 1980, when he became the *Daily Mirror* Junior Brain of Britain. He is being presented with his trophy and prizes by the actor Peter O'Toole and the TV personality Valerie Singleton. *(Author's Collection)*

Rowley Regis Secondary Modern School for Boys (Britannia Road) was very democratic when deciding who should be the school cricket captain, and so a general election was held on 16 February 1950. Here we see a lad casting his vote at the No. 1 Polling Station, with the events presided over by the headmaster, George Arthur Willetts, and Will Brittain, the teacher to his left. *(Author's Collection)*

The girls of Siviter's Lane have been busy in the handicrafts department, making a new Mayoral Pennant to be used in official duties. Embroidered with the Rowley Regis coat of arms, it is being presented to the mayor and mayoress, Councillor and Mrs Jack Shakespeare, watched over by the headmistress, Miss Maud Westwood, early 1960s. *(Maud Shaw)*

Mr G.T. Lloyd, headmaster of Rowley Regis Grammar School, and a visiting headteacher from Davenport, USA, who stayed for six months, together with Mr Geoffrey Lardner, who became the Principal of Rowley College, following the retirement of Mr Lloyd and the changes in the educational set-up, early 1970s. *(Author's Collection)*

A scene from the 1962 production of *Pygmalion* by Rowley Regis Grammar School. The cast includes, left to right: Carol Batson, -?-, Jacqueline Harper, Pamela Dudley, Keith Bradley, -?-, Gail Keefe, Paul Tilley, Anthony Wright, Carol ?, Anthony Smith, Peter Southall, Susan Dunn, Brian Davies, Nanette Hindby, Richard Baker, Jean Davis, Barbara Bootton, -?-. *(Jean Ward)*

Mr Alan Payne, the headmaster, takes the pupils at Powke Lane back in time, as the school celebrated its centenary in 1979. (*Author's Collection*)

George Arthur Willetts was headmaster at Rowley Regis Secondary School for boys from 1940 to 1960. On 16 December 1960 he was given a retirement present from the governors, staff, old boys and friends. Left to right: Councillor N.E. Thorne (chairman of governors), Alderman D. Gilbert JP (mayor of Rowley Regis), Mr G.A. Willetts, Mrs Gilbert, Mrs Willetts. (*Author's Collection*)

A scene from the 1955/6 Rowley Regis Grammar School production of *Carmen*, which was produced by Mr G.T. Lloyd (headmaster) and Mr Ernest Hancox (musical director). The ragamuffins from the first year are, left to right: Ruth Betteridge, Sheila Cartwright, -?-, Sadie Williams, -?-, Carol Bates, Isabel Dunn, Val Oldfield and Daryl Robinson; sitting: Joy Parsons, Sandra Candlelent, Sandra Mitchell, Joan Trevis, Rosalind Whyley, Mary Tilley and Gillian Sidaway. One of the boys at the front is David Smith. The girl on the steps at back was Mr Lloyd's daughter, but the names of the three principals and the soldiers are unknown. *(Joy Jones)*

A group of girls at Rowley Grammar School in the playground, which includes Jean Davies, Vera Hadlington, Susan Nicklin, Gwen Harrold and Margaret Duncan, 1962. *(Jean Ward)*

Group 3 at Wright's Lane Infant School, 1920s. *(Horace Wilson)*

Eileen Westwood, head girl of Siviter's Lane Girls' School, is being presented with a bible by the vicar of Rowley Regis, the Revd S.B. Coley, in St Giles' Church, mid-1950s. The headmistress, Miss Maud Westwood, is observing the proceedings. (*Maud Shaw*)

Above and below: Practically the whole of Siviter's Lane Girls' School, together with parents and friends, on the platform at Rowley Regis station, as they wait for the specially chartered train to take them on the school outing to Windsor and a boat trip on the River Thames, 1951. There are so many people present that the line of girls stretched the length of the platform beyond the road bridge. *(Maud Shaw)*

Gladys Troman (secretary) and Miss M.E.R. Tubb (headmistress) in the school office of Springfield Junior School, early 1960s. *(Don Parkes)*

Four of the chief prize-winners at the annual prize-giving at Rowley County Secondary Girls' School (Siviter's Lane), in 1952. Left to right: June Rose, Joyce Phipps, Dorothy Parkes and June Lowe. The prizes were distributed by Alderman Lewis Davies, Chairman of Staffordshire County Council, and the event was presided over by Councillor Albert Westwood, the Mayor of Rowley Regis and Chairman of the School Governors. *(Maud Shaw)*

The staff of Rowley Regis Grammar School, *c.* 1953. Back row, left to right: Mr E. Davies, Mr Williams, Mr Johnstone, Mr Smallwood, -?-, Mr Gwyn Jones, Mr F. Laukner, Mr Nicholls, Mr R. Stuckey, Mr E. Hancox, Mr J. Bent, Mr D.H. Watts. Front row: Mrs Hurley, -?-, Miss Richmond, Miss A.M. Harrison, Mr G.T. Lloyd (headmaster), Mr J.L. Jones, Mrs R. Hewitt, Miss N. Harrold, Miss E. Eld. *(Author's Collection)*

The Group 1 class at Knowle School, Springfield, early twentieth century. *(Derek Sale)*

The staff basketball team from Britannia Road School, *c.* 1963. Left to right: A. Wells, I. Southall, K. Savine, J. Walton, W. Landles, -?-, T.E. Jones. *(Ivan Southall)*

The staff at Britannia Road School, 1960/1. Back row, left to right: J. Mort, C. Woodward, W. Easthope, G. Jordan, E. Taylor, H. Wyle, W. Landless. Middle row: K. Thomas, R. Law, I. Southall, W. Tromans, G. Barnett, T. Jones, A. Wells, A. Green, A. Lloyd. Front row: A. Parsons, J. Walton, Mrs Hall (secretary), F.E. Sidaway (deputy head), D.J. Greville (headmaster), Mrs C. Woodward (secretary), W. Brittain, A. Johnson, N. Neale. *(Ivan Southall)*

The Youth Club of Siviter's Lane Girls School, 1950. Seated in the centre of the front row are the headmistress, Miss Westwood, and the Chairman of the Governors, Councillor Albert Westwood. *(Maud Shaw)*

Sports Day at Rowley Hall Junior School, 1970s. The houses in the immediate background are on Windsor Road, with Turner's Hill providing the backdrop. *(Author's Collection)*

Revered by generations of pupils, the band of dinner ladies from Rowley Hall Junior School take centre stage. *(Elsie Tranter)*

The football team, Rowley Regis Grammar School, 1955/6. Back row, left to right: Mr R. Stuckey, John Clift, ? Dunn, ? Wilde, Ant Nock, Des Tromans, Ant Cartwright, Alan Hale. Front row: Ant Johnson, John Witton, John (Jock) Smith, Ivan Southall, Stu Russell. *(Ivan Southall)*

The staff at Britannia Road School, 1962. Back row, left to right: J. Easthope, C. Woodward, J. Mort, -?-, D. Harris, P. Skeldon, A. Johnson, R. Jones, A. Green, G. Barnett, E. Thomas, M. Rhodes, R. Law, I. Southall. Front row: Mrs C. Easthope (secretary), W. Tromans, A. Vaughan, F.E. Sidaway (deputy head), D.J. Greville (head), J. Walton, J. Wraith, A. Parsons, Mrs D. Round (secretary). *(Ivan Southall)*

The dinner ladies at Knowle Infant School are hard at work in the kitchens, 1956. Left to right: Florence Slater, -?-, Mary Harrold and Lily Griffiths. *(Author's Collection)*

The staff at Oakham Primary School, 1972/3. Back row, left to right: Rita West, Mrs Argust (pianist), Bryan Jones, Phil Jones, Jean Bolton. Middle row: Joan Keightley, Carol Shakespeare, Pat Grainger, Wendy Williams, Mrs Randell (remedial), Cynthia Emson (non-teaching assistant), Moira Schofield. Front row: Esme Crosby, Tim O'Mara, David Eades (deputy head), Mr R.D. Worton (head), Mrs M. Reed, Mrs B. Worton, Mrs A. Gray (secretary). *(David Eades)*

Tividale School football team, 1934/5. (*Thelma Plant*)

Miss Mary E.R. Tubb, headmistress of Knowle School, Springfield, for many years, shown in 1969, a few years before her retirement. Many pupils remember her with affection, although at the same time recall her being a rather strict disciplinarian. (*Don Parkes*)

3

Church & Chapel

A rare picture of the second St Giles' Church, late nineteenth century. The original church, which had stood on virtually the same site from 1199 to 1840, was replaced with this distinctive Victorian building complete with ornate tower. *(Edna Parkes)*

A view of the ruins of the fire-damaged St Giles' Church, 1913. *(Malcolm Whitehouse)*

The interior of the ruins of the fire-ravaged church as an assessment is undertaken to see what damage has been caused, 1913. The local constable is on hand to ensure that all is calm. *(Ken Rock)*

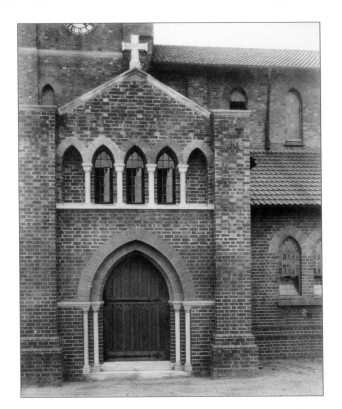

The south-west porch was added to St Giles' Church in the 1920s, and was dedicated by the Assistant Bishop of Birmingham, Hamilton Baynes, on 29 September 1926. One of its striking architectural features is the parvise or upper room, which revived a tradition in many ancient churches. *(Malcolm Warby)*

A group of ladies from St Giles' Church have just paraded from the church, down to Rowley Village and turned into Mackmillan Road, to join others in a joint service in Britannia Park, early 1960s. *(David Eades)*

The first bells were introduced to the original St Giles' Church as early as 1684, and in the subsequent churches there has continued a fine tradition of campanology. In the early 1980s a new bell was introduced into the peal. Taking a break from the hard work we see ringers Brian Darby, Leslie Bird, Michael Vine and Alan Roberts. *(Leslie Bird)*

St Giles' Church has a fine record of campanology. These four local lads are in the belltower taking a lesson from Ezra Homer, then aged about seventy, in 1948. The boys are left to right Joe Chater, Jim Sidaway, Tony Perry and Fred Willetts. The ringers were affiliated to the Worcestershire & District Change Ringers Association, whose certificate is on the wall behind them. *(Fred Willetts)*

The Birmingham Road Sunday School contingent parading up Limes Avenue to join the ladies shown on page 57 for the assembly in the park, early 1960s. David Evans and Arthur Wood are carrying the banner; one of the ribbons is held by Anita Page. Tom Aldridge is seen leading scholars, with John Johnson and Ivor Harris on the left. *(Anthony Page)*

D. Parkes del. 1803.

The above is a S.W. view of the parish church of Rowley Regis, co. Stafford. It is a very irregular building & consists of a nave, chancel, & side aisle to the South, divided from the nave by clumsy gothic pillars & pointed arches. The font is of very rude workman-ship. On the N.W. side the Church Yard is a large bone house, or Charnel house, now filled with human bones. The Church standing on an elevated spot, there is an extensive prospect from the Ch: Yard.

Font in Rowley church.

A postcard of a drawing made by the acclaimed Hill & Cakemore artist, David Parkes, of the first St Giles' Church, and its Norman font. The original drawing is now in the British Museum. The contemporary description gives us a useful impression of the ancient edifice, none of which remains today. *(CHAS)*

St Giles' Church football team, 1913/14. The vicar is the Revd A.F. Dauglish. In the middle row in front of the goalkeeper is Samuel Taylor, who was killed in action at Ephey on 1 April 1917 while serving in 1/7 Battalion, Worcestershire Regiment, B Company, no. 7 platoon. In a letter home he had written that many of the men in this team had been lost in action. (Derek Sale)

The Revd Alfred Dye, the Minister of Providence Strict and Particular Baptist Church, Bell End, is seen outside the manse, which was next to the church, c. 1910. (Jim Beasley)

Inside the Crematorium in Powke Lane, at the official opening ceremony, held in the mid-1960s. Some of the dignitaries who can be seen are the Revd. T. Leslie Haywood (minister of Blackheath Congregational Church), the Mayor of Rowley Regis (councillor Vic Wakeman), the Bishop of Birmingham (Rt Revd L. Wilson), the Revd John Farmer (vicar of St Paul's, Blackheath), the Revd S. Bernard Coley (vicar of St Giles', Rowley Regis). *(Malcolm Warby)*

Members of Knowle Methodist Church celebrate the opening of their new schoolroom with a party in 1954. *(Ken Biggs)*

The lych gate of St Giles' Church, opposite the top of Park Avenue, Church Road. On the left is the verger's cottage, which was also used as a Sunday School in the time of George Beese. *(Derek Crump)*

Canon Guy Rogers giving the opening address at a garden party held in the grounds of the old vicarage of St Giles' Church, in the 1930s. *(Author's Collection)*

The Revd John T. Hughes was born in Rowley Regis and was ordained as a Methodist minister. A widely travelled man, he held appointments around the country, including a period in the Isle of Man. In his younger days he was a talented footballer, and had a trial for Aston Villa. *(Jean Bubb)*

The Revd Herbert Card was one of the longest serving vicars of St Giles' Church; he is pictured here in 1931. In addition to his church duties he was also involved in local politics, serving on Rowley Regis council, and acting as mayor of the borough. *(Malcolm Warby)*

The scholars of the Endowed School, Rowley Village, celebrate their Sunday School Anniversary, 1954. *(Philip Adams)*

Adults and children from Knowle Methodist Church preparing to take the final curtain of their Christmas Show, early 1960s. *(Ken Biggs)*

The Revd S. Bernard Coley takes the place of honour at the top table at a dinner held in the church hall of St Giles' Church, *c.* 1965. It was probably a dinner to launch a stewardship campaign. *(Malcolm Warby)*

The bell ringers at St Giles' Church, early 1980s. They are Judith Russell (vicar's daughter), Brian Darby, Brian Faulkner, David Chiswell, Leslie Bird, Michael Vine, Alan and Gill Roberts, Les and Sandra Wilson. *(Leslie Bird)*

The original premises of Knowle Methodist Church, Dudley Road, Springfield, late nineteenth century. *(Ken Biggs)*

The Revd M. Neville Kearney, MA, the vicar of St Giles' from 1893, with his wife and family. *(Malcolm Warby)*

Today, as you travel up Rowley Hill at night, St Giles' Church makes an impressive sight, silhouetted against the dark sky. Here it is shown illuminated by gaslight, 26 October 1934. *(Author's Collection)*

Some of the young children from St Giles' in a pageant being judged for the best costume, 12 July 1986. In the centre are church workers Mrs Woolvin, with her daughter Anthea. *(Derek Crump)*

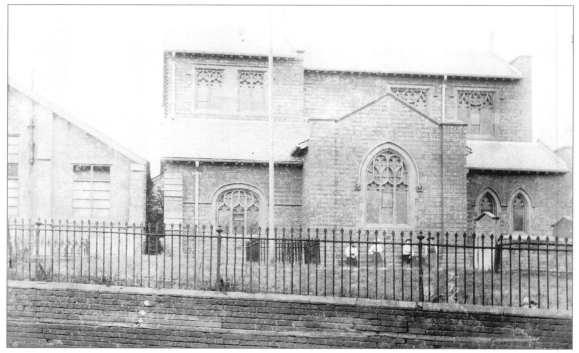

A group of cleaning ladies, partially hidden by the railings, pose outside the building of the fourth and current St Giles', *c.* 1920–3. The hut on the left occupies the position of the rebuilt tower. *(Ken Rock)*

4

The World of Work

Looking down into one of the massive quarry excavations, while the removal of Rowley Rag stone was still in full production. *(Derek Crump)*

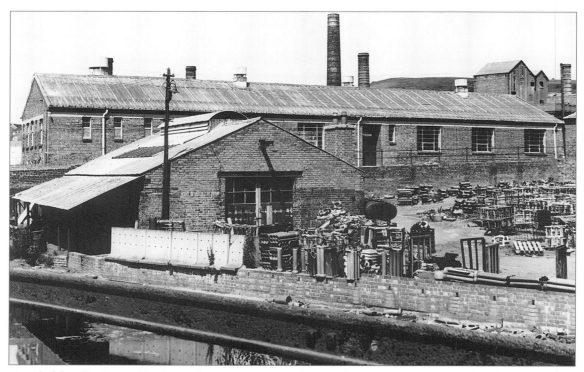

Founded by Sir Henry Doulton, the sanitary-ware factory bearing his name produced much of the pipework and sanitary fittings for the whole of the West Midlands area. In so doing, it also provided work for generations of local people, who were already skilled in working in areas such as brick-making, which required many of the same skills. Here is part of the factory and canal side storage yard. *(CHAS)*

Rowley Regis is at the southern-most tip of the famous 30ft South Staffordshire coal field (which gives rise to the term Black Country). It was a typical Staffordshire mining community, which had many small privately owned pits. One of the larger collieries in this district was Rowley Hall, and this is the scene at the pit head in 1900. *(CHAS)*

Long since disappeared from Rowley are these coke ovens, *c.* 1900. *(CHAS)*

Rowley people loved to take trips away from their locality, and most of the major employers organised regular outings. This jolly group, who took their own entertainment with the accordion player, was from T.W. Lench, *c.* 1950. The only person identified is Harold Wilfred Cole, who is on the front row, third from the right. *(David Eades)*

Sir Henry Maybury presents a Gold Medal for extra long service of seventy years to George Taylor, who had started working at the Hailstone Quarry at the tender age of nine. Standing behind Sir Henry is Jim Troman, dressed in plus fours, who was the manager at the site. *(Derek Sale)*

The factory entrance to Doulton's works, with the company offices. *(CHAS)*

One of the several firms supplying bread and cakes to the area was Harris', their bakehouse being situated in Bell End, between Park Avenue and Newhall Road. Here George Tromans is shown with the firm's van on his delivery round, posing outside the entrance to Corngreaves Hall, in the 1940s. *(Ivan Southall)*

One of the ovens at Doulton's works. It was established in 1848 for the manufacture of drainpipes, but it also made architectural terracotta and blue bricks, later concentrating on the production of glazed sanitary ware. The factory eventually ceased production and closed in 1979. The site is presently occupied by an industrial estate. *(CHAS)*

The staff at Warley Fasteners, a subsidiary firm of T.W. Lench, in festive mood for Queen Elizabeth II's Silver Jubilee in 1977. Left to right: Edna Walker, Dora Good, Gertie Rock, May Lloyd and Amy Jones. *(May Lloyd)*

A group of Doulton's pensioners on an outing: the location and identity of the participants is not known. *(David Sadler)*

A group of quarry workers, similarly anonymous. *(Gordon Parsons)*

An early aerial view of the premises of T.W. Lench, at the end of the First World War. The area in the foreground is the reclaimed pit workings, at one time known as The Totnalls, which was turned into extensive recreation grounds. The fields at the back show that the residential area of the Mackmillan Estate had yet to be developed. *(Linda George)*

The T.W. Lench ex-servicemen gather to plant trees in 1973 to commemorate the completion of twenty-five years service with the company of Managing Director Robert Lench. It also marked twenty-five years since the founding of the Ex-servicemen's Association. Among those present are Robert Lench, Bill Mallin, Arthur Payne, Les Eley and Ted Baker. *(Dorothy Tolley)*

The Rowley & Springfield Despatch Fund for Miners' Kiddies Tea, at Knowle Methodist Sunday School, *c.* 1913. Mr and Mrs Priest are on the left, and Beatrice Dunn (later Biggs) is on the right. *(Ray Whitehouse)*

The buildings at the top of one of the many quarries, early twentieth century. *(CHAS)*

The frontispiece from a catalogue of products made by T.W. Lench, 1926. At the time there were over 1,200 workers, who had more than a mile of specialised machinery to manufacture all kinds of fastening materials. *(Graham Allen)*

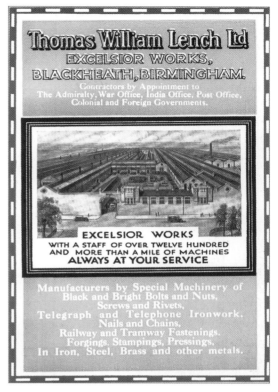

Workers of all ages at a local nut and bolt manufacturer are seen displaying just a few of their products, early twentieth century. They may have belonged to a subsidiary firm of T.W. Lench, but this is not certain. *(Author's Collection)*

Tom Dudley (whose parents kept the fish and chip shop next to the George and Dragon in High Street) and David Sadler are taking a rest from making gullies at Doultons Works, early 1930s. In this large workshop there were only three workers, who made everything by hand. In this particular shop they made the underground brown ware, rather than the more familiar white sanitary fixtures. *(David Sadler)*

A large group of workers at Warley Fasteners celebrate the Silver Jubilee in 1977 in patriotic style. Among the crowd are Margie ?, Rosie Griffiths, Carrie Hickman, May Lloyd, Pat ?, Gladys Hughes and Edith ?. The solitary man at the back is John Brookes. *(May Lloyd)*

Brothers Harry and Billy Skidmore take a moment out from their busy schedule on Throne Farm, perhaps the largest in the area. The site is now part of the Lion Farm housing estate. *(Graham Beasley)*

Inside the oliver shop at T.W. Lench, just prior to it being dismantled and taken to the Black Country Living Museum, April 1977. *(Ron Moss)*

The colliery yard at Rowley Hall, with its chimney, winding gear and iron and wooden trucks at the pit head, *c.* 1900. *(CHAS)*

The Rowley Regis Ambulance Brigade, 1923. *(Freda Green)*

Led by Bill Mallin and Ernest Payne,
T.W. Lench's ex-servicemen enter Powke
Lane cemetery on 11 November to pay
their respects to twenty-seven fallen
comrades from the Second World War
and the dead from other conflicts.
(Dorothy Tolley)

Another group of Rowley quarry workers.
(Author's Collection)

This time clock at T.W. Lench could no doubt tell many tales, if only it could speak, of the thousands of local workers who have clocked on over the years. *(Ron Moss)*

The Blackheath firm of coach builders, Everton's of Long Lane, adapted all kinds of vehicles. This hearse was made for F.P. Gaunt & Sons in the early 1950s. *(Robert Everton)*

5

People & Events

Members of Rowley Urban District Council, 1933. Left to right: Councillors Herbert Grainger, Thomas Price, Benjamin Hobbs, Thomas Willetts, Enoch Read, John Percival Pennington, Miss Sarah Elizabeth Wesley, William H. Blunt, David Matthew Chapman, Albert Henry Hancock and Thomas Evans Walton. *(CHAS)*

The Guest family of Rowley Regis including George (baby), Anne, Arthur, John and Violet. In the middle of the back row is the well-known character Joe the lamplighter. *(Irene Davies)*

Some mothers and babies from Rowley visit the Midland Counties Dairy, Birmingham during Baby Week, early 1920s. *(Eileen Johnson)*

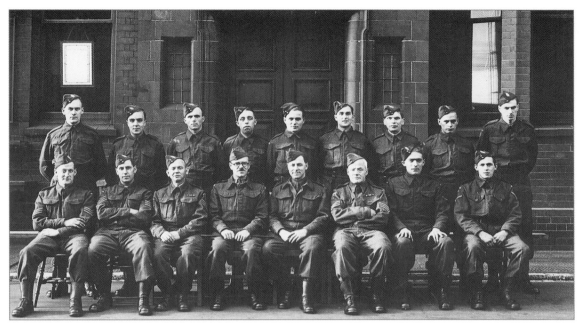

A contingent of the Rowley Regis Home Guard. Jim Harrold is on the far left of the front row. *(Margaret Sheward)*

Local children dressed up for the VE celebrations in Bell End, in front of the old cottages opposite the bottom of Park Avenue, 1945. Those identified include Marilyn and Philip Bannister, Irene Hill, Pat and Mary Gaunt, Joyce ?, Jean Grove, Geoffrey Grant, Jean Davies and James and Anthony Page. *(Author's Collection)*

Britannia Park Nursery children and staff relax during the summer of 1948. Roger Wellens is on the lap of the nursery nurse on the far left, Michael Bowater is second from the right, and the lady in the white blouse in the centre of the back row is Miss Taylor. *(Brian Wellens)*

George Ruston, born in 1884, was the son of Joseph Ruston, the founder of Ebenezer Baptist Chapel. He trained at West Bromwich School of Art, winning a scholarship to study in London, and became a renowned sculptor, working initially at Doulton's in Rowley Regis. He emigrated to America, where he was similarly employed in New York. Then he became a deacon in the American Baptist Church, founding many churches both in the United States and Canada, and edited the periodical published by the church. *(Linda George)*

The staff of the Britannia Park Nursery, 1948. Iris Wellens is second on the left in the back row, and to her left is Miss Taylor. The lady in charge, Mrs Whihall, is in the centre of the front row. *(Brian Wellens)*

Throne Crescent residents celebrate VE Day, 1945. Those present included Margaret and Jean Walters, Sheila and Jimmy Gould, Geraldine Partington, Barbara and Brian Billington, Donald Hinton, Edith Taylor, Mrs Taylor, Mrs Danks and Mary, Mrs Perry and family, Mrs Smith and Rita. *(Margaret Newman)*

James and Elizabeth Slater pose in the front garden of their cottage in Rowley Village, late 1950s. The premises of the Steelace Company can clearly be seen in the background, and at one time Mrs Slater was a cleaner in the works. *(Mary Cutler)*

Some of the children from Throne Road, all dressed up to celebrate the Coronation of Queen Elizabeth II, 1953. Included are Alan Hadley (fourth from left), Peter Simpson (fifth from left), and Trevor and Ivan Jones. *(Margaret Hadley/David Eades)*

The old cottages in Springfield Lane make a fitting backdrop for Jack and Sarah Howard with their new motor bike, *c.* 1930. *(Bob Grosvenor)*

A group of locals with their dogs outside the Kings Arms public house, situated in the older part of Rowley Village, late 1930s. *(Gordon Parsons)*

Firemen battled for more than two hours to try to save Lowe's Timber Yard in Waterfall Lane, on Sunday 6 June 1976. Flames reached heights of 80ft and caused damage of more than £200,000. At the time more than fifty people were employed by the firm, which had been in business for eighty years. *(Ron Wood)*

Mark Nock (1846–1927) was born in Rowley Village. He first worked as a nailer, but he soon moved into coal mining, an industry in which he remained until retirement, working his way up from labourer to pit bank manager. In his spare time he was a dedicated Methodist, and acted as Sunday School superintendent at Zion's Hill Church for many years. *(Kath Mole)*

A splendid family portrait of Harry and Sarah Lench and their six children, early twentieth century. Harry, who was awarded the OBE, is at the back with Harry Jnr; Lillian (a JP), Sarah and Mary are in the centre, seated; Nellie, Alfred William and Thomas Charles complete the group. *(Linda George)*

The Blackheath Company of the Home Guard, pictured at Turner's Hill, 1940. Back row, left to right: A. Holmes, -?-, J. Evans, G. Jenkins, A. Tibbetts (sergeant). Front row: G. Parkes, F. Kimberlin, L. Bird, F. Payne. *(Leslie Bird)*

Members of the Rowley Pigeon Fanciers' Club, clutching their obligatory flat caps, on one of their outings. James Devonport is among the crowd. *(Eileen Johnson)*

Soldiers posing with their recently acquired machine guns during the First World War. Arthur Payne, a resident of Limes Avenue, is the first on the left in the front row. After the war he was a long-term employee of T.W. Lench. *(Dorothy Tolley)*

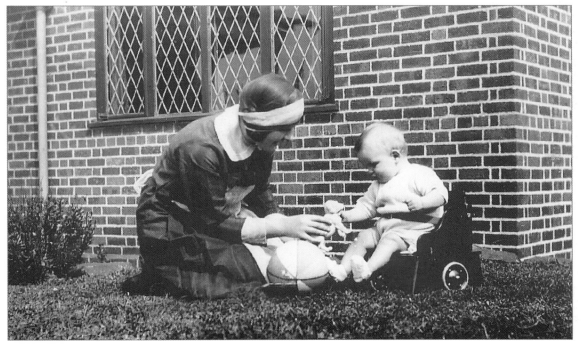

Jeremy Beasley, the grandson of the popular Rowley doctor, Dr James Griffin Beasley, is being looked after by his nurse, Doris Devonport, in the family garden in Siviter's Lane, 1930s. *(Eileen Johnson)*

Three local girls, Doris Adams, May Gaunt and Joyce Cooper, who 'did their bit' during the Second World War by joining the Auxiliary Fire Service, 1943. *(May Botfield)*

Enjoying a dip in the crowded Britannia Park Paddling Pool, summer 1936. Left to right: Joan Tromans, Margaret Holland, -?-, Betty Holland. *(Betty Johnson)*

The inscription on the cart reads 'William Andrews, Rowley Regis', in this idyllic rural scene from the early twentieth century. The workers are pictured gathering in the hay at Warley Abbey Farm, but whether the carter and his helpers are from Rowley or from the farm is not certain. *(Author's Collection)*

Members of the Church in the Garden (an independent church founded by Walter Darby in his house) prepare to go out to distribute literature, and are seen outside a house in Ross. The group includes Walter Darby, the pastor on the far right, and Rose Dovey, second from the left. *(Martin Pearson)*

Rowley Regis Fire Brigade, *c*. 1920. Among those identified are, back row: H. Green (second from right), Mr Fendall (seventh from right), H. Baynham (eighth from right); third row: A. Cook (first from right), Mr Knott (fourth from right); second row: J. Cook, second in charge (first from right); R. Fendall (fourth

from right), Mr Salt (eighth from right), Mr Longfellow, chief sanitary inspector and commander of the Fire Brigade (ninth from right); front row: councillor and ex-MP Mr C. Sitch (far left), Councillor Thornton (far right). *(Freda Green)*

Ray Bridgewater with some of his prize-winning onions, in his allotment at the top of Britannia Park. *(Ray Bridgewater)*

The mayoral party outside St Giles' Church, May 1984. Behind the mayor's sergeant are Geoff Hadley, town clerk, Councillor and Mrs Jack Smith and Councillor and Mrs Walker. *(Freda Smith)*

Children in fancy dress wait on a make-shift platform in Uplands Avenue to be judged for the prize in the Coronation competition. Those taking part are Pauline and Olive White, Adrian Kenyon, Judith Dallow, Christine Griffin, David Nightingale, David Griffin, Gillian Mades, Brian Roberts and Iris Richards. It is not known who won. *(John Dallow)*

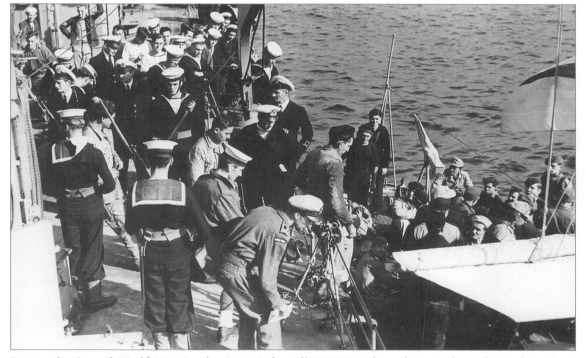

During the Second World War Rowley Regis 'adopted' HMS *Tumult*, and received regular updates from the captain. Included in one of his letters was this photograph showing German PoWs who had been captured from ships in the Dalmatian Islands in September 1943, disembarking at an Italian port. *(Author's Collection)*

To mark the granting of the charter recognising Rowley Regis as an Urban District Council, a celebration was held on 28 September 1933, including a procession around the perimeter of the borough. *Above*: C. Buckley (town clerk), Ben Hobbs (charter mayor), the Revd Herbert Card, Councillor E. Read, R. Johnson (mace-bearer) and Alderman D.N. Chapman at the rear of the the Municipal Offices in Lawrence Lane. *Below*: The procession is taking leave of Old Hill on the way to Blackheath and Rowley. *(CHAS)*

A party held in Uplands Avenue to mark the Coronation celebrations of Queen Elizabeth II, 1953. Among those identified are Mr and Mrs Griffin, Mr and Mrs Kenyon, Mr and Mrs Smith, Mr and Mrs Dallow, Mr Hall, Ann Leek, Joan Walton, Mrs Gower, Mr. Lappage, Mrs Underhill, Mr and Mrs Kaye and Mrs May Walton. *(John Dallow)*

Frederick T. Wilson, the secretary of the Education Committee of the newly formed Borough of Rowley Regis, 1930s. *(Horace Wilson)*

George Whittall with his wife Martha outside their home in Limes Avenue, *c.* 1930. He was one of several of his family who were proud members of the Rowley Regis Fire Service, and George is seen wearing his uniform. He was one of the officers who attended the fire at St Giles' Church in 1913. *(David Hickman)*

Throne Crescent residents, in common with many others, held a street party to commemorate the Coronation in 1953. Among those present were Margaret and Jean Walters, Sheila and Jimmy Gould, Geraldine Partington, Ann Darby, Margaret Westwood, Margaret and Madge Insker, Pauline and Brian Johnson, Pat and Beatrice Cooper, Janet Adams, John and Eric Winwood, Donald and Dorothy Mincock, Maurice Bishop, Malcolm Ruddall, Leonard Bricknall, Adrian and Judith Church and Beryl Barton. *(Margaret Newman)*

The bowls team which met in Britannia Park, with William Henry Walters, a long-time worker at BTH Ltd, checking the scores, 1970s. *(Margaret Newman)*

Local children are seen perched on the boot of an Austin Cambridge, which is parked on the driveway of 22 Bell End, at the bottom of Park Avenue, *c.* 1948. Left to right: Marilyn Bannister, Philip Bannister, Alan Baggott, Robert Baggott and Philip Adams. *(Philip Adams)*

James Brinton with his son Reg and the family dog are seen in their garden at 22 Bell End, 1920s. The large building in the background is the Providence Strict and Particular Baptist Chapel, and on the right are the old cottages in Bell End, demolished to make way for the council housing. *(Philip Adams)*

Aston Villa and England footballer Tommy Smart, with his daughter Gwen Jameson, grandson Paul Jameson and a young friend in the Sir Robert Peel public house, *c.* 1960. *(Paul Jameson)*

John Percival Pennington, Mayor of the old Urban District Council of Rowley Regis, a position he held for two years in the mid-1940s. He also served in various capacities with Staffordshire County Council and local hospitals, being an original member of the Dudley and Stourbridge Hospital Management Committee. In addition he was a local magistrate for many years, serving as chairman of the Rowley Regis Justices. He was married to Gladys for over sixty years and lived in Birmingham Road. *(Jean Ward)*

Members of Rowley Regis Horticultural Society pose by their magnificent display of vegetables, which was entered in the Inter-Borough Competition in the late 1960s. *(CHAS)*

FIRST PRIZE EXHIBIT ROWLEY REGIS HORTICULTURAL SOCIETY INTER. BOROUGH COMPETITION

Three young members of the 1st Rowley Scouts at their Annual Camp at Woolacombe, Devon, August 1953. They are seen practising their culinary skills as they attempt to cook a rasher of bacon attached to a piece of string over the embers of the camp fire. *(Derek Crump)*

George Beese was verger and sexton at St Giles' Church, serving under three vicars, for over forty years. He was highly regarded by all who knew him, and had a masterful knowledge of the many complicated relationships within Rowley families, knowing the location of everybody's family grave sites. In his cottage, situated next to the church, he ran a Sunday school for many years. He died after a short illness on 21 April 1965, in his sixty-fifth year. *(Elsie Tranter)*

One of the many coach outings enjoyed by Rowley folk back in the 1920s, although where this particular trip ended up is not known. Mrs Olive Holland is near the back of the charabanc with her son George, and others recognised are Mrs Bird with her son Stan, Liz Hale and her daughter Sally, and the baby being held high is May Gaunt. Mrs Mary Ann Horton is at the front, next to her friend Mrs Dingley. (*Betty Johnson*)

The Sandwell Civic Procession, which has left St Giles' Church, passed down Rowley Village and is seen here turning right from Bell End into Britannia Road, 1984. The mayor, Councillor Jack Smith, is walking with the town clerk, Geoff Hadley, followed by the deputy mayor, Councillor Walker, the local MP, Peter Archer QC, Councillor Joe Adams and Councillor Dr Hiron Roy. (*Freda Smith*)

Led by the band of the 1st Rowley Scouts, the Civic Parade passes the saluting base in Charles Avenue, May 1985. The mayor, Councillor Derek Crump (who was a long-term member of the Scouts), is seen taking the salute, and to the right of the dais are the deputy mayor and mayoress, Councillor and Mrs Melia, the mayor's sergeant, Sam Copson, and Mr and Mrs Peter Archer QC, MP. *(Derek Crump)*

Thelma Plant, Elizabeth Troman, Alan Plant and Ella Bird (also known as Bessie) outside Hailstone House, in Tippity Green. *(Peter Goddard)*

Dan Timmings and John Bird on the steps outside 37 Tippity Green, *c.* 1950. Mr Bird was the licensee of the Kings Arms public house in Rowley Village, having previously been the captain of Walsall Town FC in the 1920s. *(Thelma Plant)*

William and David Brettell, with their cousin Robert Stokes, at the rear of 5 Siviter's Lane, where William and David lived with their parents and grandparents, Richard and Nancy Hodgetts, *c.* 1949. Nancy was the proprietor of a draper's shop. *(Chris Brettell)*

The Stone family in their garden at 133 Rowley Village, where they are preparing for action with gas-mask drill, *c.* 1941. The two older girls are Betty and Dorothy, and Judy and Marie are at the front. *(Judy Hall)*

Some of the residents of Bell End celebrating VE Day in 1945. Among those present are Lily Grove, Margaret Adams and Miriam Baggott. *(Philip Adams)*

Another view of the boating lake in Britannia Park, *c.* 1936. In the boat (left to right) are Suie Gaunt (now Downing, living in Australia), Margaret Holland, Betty Holland, Barbara Lowe and one of their friends. *(Betty Holland)*

ROWLEY REGIS WAR MEMORIAL.   "EDITH CAVELL" AMBULANCE.

After the First World War it was decided to erect a war memorial as a tribute to local people killed in the conflict, so various public subscription events were organised, including a Flag Day on 11 October 1919. In addition to the memorial, funds were also sought to purchase this ambulance, named after the famous nurse who worked in the trenches, at the cost of £195. *(Anthony Johnson)*

Proudly displaying the latest in both fashion and bicycles is this young woman about town, Lois Eliza Harrold. She was born in 1880, and married Joseph Edward Partridge in 1904. Her mother was a member of the Ruston family, the founders of Ebenezer Baptist Chapel in Hawes Lane. *(Yvonne Grant)*

Three long-term friends from Rowley Village, left to right, Jimmy Smith, John Parkes and Dan Bennett, all called up to serve in the First World War, 1917. After the war Dan kept the Village Fish and Chip shop for many years. *(Ray Parkes)*

Rowley Regis folk sponsored the building of this Spitfire to help the war effort between 1939 and 1945. It was built in Castle Bromwich, and had the serial number P7732, entering service on 7 December 1940, and at one time it was part of the squadron commanded by the legendary Douglas Bader. It was damaged several times before being taken out of commission, and presumably scrapped, on 5 June 1945. *(Author's Collection)*

William Bridgewater, seen here in the 1890s, was a well-known figure in Rowley Village. He was the father of a large family, and in spite of having only one arm was renowned as a maker of all types of ladders. *(Ray Bridgewater)*

Margaret (standing) and Minnie Brinton of 22 Bell End, the youngest children of James and Laura Brinton (née Taylor), early 1920s. *(Philip Adams)*

A large group of guests gather to celebrate the wedding of Matthew Siviter and Cissie Price in the front garden of 50 Hawes Lane, 17 September 1927. The ceremony had taken place at St Giles' Church. *(Derek Siviter)*

The children of engineer and shopkeeper, William and Betsy Mallin of 1 Bell End. Left to right: Sarah Jane (born 5 August 1888), William Ernest (born 17 October 1895) and Ethel Maud (born 26 May 1892). In later life Sarah took over the family grocer shop, Maud became a teacher at Siviter's Lane School for Girls, and Bill worked at T.W. Lench (see pages 77 and 83). *(Author's Collection)*

Standing beside the recently erected memorial to Joseph Walters and family in the churchyard of St Giles' Church, are Bill and Ann Dowell, 1900s. *(Edna Parkes)*

These two wedding pictures taken at the entrance to St Giles' Church show the differences in fashion and cars. The old cottages of Church Road are clearly visible in the background. *Above*: The wedding of Thelma Woodhouse and George Raymond Plant, 10 November 1951. *(Thelma Plant)*
Below: The wedding of Gladys May Harrold and John Thomas (known as Jack) Troman, 18 October 1947. Jack and Gladys were stalwart members of the Baptist Chapel in Bell End. *(Gladys Troman)*

A young Jimmy Stone outside an Anderson shelter in the back garden of 133 Rowley Village,
c. 1941. *(Judy Hall)*

Jack Willetts with his daughter Patricia on the 'fowd' of 4 Siviter's Lane, 1947. The large pear tree on the right is in the Post Office garden in Rowley Village, which sold the fruit at 2d per lb. Any windfalls fell 10ft into the garden of Bade and Annie Philpott, who passed them to local children via a basket tied to a line stump. According to Pat Soley, Mr Willetts tended the garden of Dr Rainsford at Mountford House, who allowed him to keep a vegetable plot there, and on one occasion the doctor cut his hand and asked Mr Willetts to stitch up the wound! *(Pat Soley)*

Walter Darby, the founder of the Church in the Garden, Ross, is seen outside the front of his house by the church notice board. *(Martin Pearson)*

ay Bridgewater (right) receives the Winner's Cup in the first County Borough of Warley Allotments ompetition, 1966. Mrs Evelyn Matthews and Reg Downing (both Rowley Regis councillors) watch as it presented by the mayor of Warley, Councillor Wilfred Carter. *(Ray Bridgewater)*

group of ladies from the Springfield area, who belonged to the Darby and Joan Class at Knowle lethodist Church, 1950s. *(Frank Taylor)*

Arthur Troman (far left) and George Knowles with two workmates and their dogs, outside the Four Ways public house in Portway Road. Arthur spent his working life at Allsop's Hill Quarry. *(Peter Goddard)*

Four of the Westwood brothers of Hawes Lane, including Cecil, who was verger of St Giles' Church, and Albert, who became a local councillor and mayor of Rowley Regis. The family were staunch Methodists, and both the named brothers were Methodist Local Preachers. *(Trevor Westwood)*

Eighteen-year-old Stanley Willetts of Mackmillan Road in front of the Wellington bomber in which he served as a navigator. Unfortunately, he was posted as missing in action after a mission that took place on the night of 18 November 1943. *(Fred Willetts)*

Jack Ingram was the son of Reuben, churchwarden at St Giles' Church, and served in the Royal Navy in the Second World War. He was serving on HMS *Prince of Wales*, which, together with its sister ship HMS *Repulse*, was attacked by eighty Japanese aircraft some 50 miles off the coast of Malaya on the night of 10 December 1941. Both ships were sunk, the *Prince of Wales* losing 327 men. Jack survived the incident and spent time in the jungle, living rough, though he never wanted to talk about the experience. *(Thelma Plant)*

Charles B. Adams in Darjeeling, India, October 1944. Lieutenant (later Captain) Adams served with the 2nd Battalion of the Royal Warwickshire Regiment. He later lived at 22 B End and was well known in the local commun serving as a magistrate between 1954 and 1970, firstly on the Rowley Regis and later on the Warley Bench. He had a long-time association with the Endowed School, Rowley Village, serving as Sunday School Superintendent for some time, and also had a furniture shop in High Street, Blackheath. *(Philip Adams)*

Arthur John Hughes, the son of John T. Hughes (see page 63), served in the Royal Air Force, and managed to survive combat duties, but unfortunately he died in an air/sea rescue exercise, on Good Friday 30 March 1945. He was required to bale out into the English Channel, and in so doing contracted pneumonia, from which he never recovered. He is buried in the churchyard at St Giles' Church. *(Jean Bubb)*

A young Dorothy Stone from Rowley Village enjoys her ride on the latest tricycle with a companion, *c.* 1927. The picture was taken in the yard behind Cashmore's shop, Birmingham Road. *(Judy Hall)*

ACKNOWLEDGEMENTS

Wherever possible acknowledgement is given for each picture, either to the original photographer, where known, or to the person loaning the photograph. Permission to use copyrighted pictures has been sought, but apologies are extended for inadvertent use of any material. Special thanks are once again extended to all the staff at Sandwell Community History and Archives Service (CHAS), to the editor and staff at the *Black Country Bugle* and to David Hickman for his introductory essay.

In such a publication there are almost certainly some errors, the text being dependent on memories related to the author, and again apologies are rendered in advance for any mistakes. Perhaps a few readers will be disappointed that some items are missing, and if there is anyone who has any photographs which may be included in future books, the author would be pleased to hear about them.